Y0-CXH-059

To _____

For your
reading pleasure
and inspiration.

From _____

HAPPINESS BEGINS
BEFORE BREAKFAST

*Thoughts on Life
and Living It More Fully*

by Harry and Joan Mier

Edited, and with a Foreword, by
GILBERT READE

Merit Publishers • Beverly Hills, California

By Harry and Joan Mier

If the Shoe Fits
Happiness Begins Before Breakfast
Building Our Own Rainbows

Eighth Printing, 1967

REVISED EDITION

©1962 by Harry and Joan Mier. *All rights reserved, including the right of reproduction in whole or in part in any form, except for short quotations in critical essays and reviews.*

MANUFACTURED IN THE UNITED STATES OF AMERICA.

Contents

⤴ *Acknowledgment* ⤵

The authors gratefully acknowledge the encouragement and helpful suggestions of Mrs. Maxwell Fields, Mr. Jim Wheeler and Mr. John Keller.

ᔕᕫ *Foreword* ᕫᔕ

In *Happiness Begins Before Breakfast,* timely and timeless truths glow anew as enduring guidelines illuminating the human journey along the Road of Life, for Harry and Joan Mier write about LIVING with extraordinary insight, depth and warmth.

Their book is refreshing—a bright ray of sunshine that succeeds in being both entertaining and inspiring. Each of these thoughts, infused with warmth and inviting kindness, aims at helping people to discern and then to direct themselves along those paths leading to lasting joy and profound inner satisfaction.

Simply and meaningfully projected, their down-to-earth observations are ever perceptive, often amusing, and frequently provocative. The authors elevate the human spirit and promote the sound sense of values they hold to be fundamental to enjoying a full, happy and worthwhile life.

Here, indeed, is a book about living, written with uncommon clarity and conviction, by two people who *know* that each day must be made a successful entity in itself right from the beginning, right from the moment of arising. Harry and Joan Mier *know* that by making it so *Happiness Begins Before Breakfast.*

—Gilbert Reade

Hollywood, California, 1966

Our manner of saluting
each new dawn, each new threshold,
and the attitudes, the will,
the enlightenment, the gifts
with which we approach each new day,
with its challenges and its opportunities,
determine in a large sense
what we will bring to the day
and what happiness
and richness of spirit
we will enjoy from it.

PART I

A Bit of Seasoning

THE BONUS

By avoiding foolish strife
And conquering your fears,
You'll add years to your life
And life to your years.

INNER RADIANCE

The more beautiful the inside
one maintains for oneself,
the more attractive the outside
he presents to others.

A FOOT IN THE DOOR

Put your best foot **forward;**
Be sure the shoe is shined.
First impressions can open
The door to another's mind.

LUCK'S LUBRICANT

By his positive thoughts and actions
a man oils his own wheel of fortune.

BEAUTY OR BONDAGE

Each event in life may add a link or a jewel,
for as we design it,
Life becomes a chain or a necklace.

LIVING MEMORIAL

The most enduring memorials
are those we build
in the hearts of our fellow men.

THE HIGH HURDLES

Although a handicap is usually an obstacle,
it need not be a barrier.
Accept it as a challenge—
that extra incentive for achieving success!

FRINGE BENEFIT

To get the most from life's span,
let the rocking chair be just another reward—
not your goal!

SURE SCALE

Purpose is only as strong
as the man who pursues it.

NOT SO EXCLUSIVE

All others cannot always be wrong,
Just as you cannot always be right.
And as not all others are dumb,
You're not the only one who's bright.

"E" FOR EFFORT

When you say you can't,
You're already done;
When you say you'll try,
You've at least begun!

THE DAWNING

The recognition of ignorance
is the first spark of enlightenment.

THE BEQUEST

What they leave *in* their children
should concern parents more
than what they'll leave *to* them!

DON'T MOVE IN YET

We've often heard it's fine to think high,
Build make-believe castles in the sky.
But you can't expect to live like a king
Until you've made your castle an earthly thing.

DETOUR

Personal progress and attainment
Are needlessly deferred
When our attention and energies
Are on trivial things conferred.

A MATTER OF CHOICE

Your mind is *yours* . . .
You can starve it or feed it,
Let it rust or oil its parts,
Narrow it with laziness
Or broaden it with usefulness—
It's up to *you!*

WHERE IT COUNTS MOST

Recognition and status are
earnestly sought by most men,
and many seek it far afield.
Yet the most rewarding forms
are the respect, honor and love
man inspires in his own home.

TURNABOUT

A man's name attaches to his words and deeds,
and these in turn will "label" the man.

THE MAGIC TOUCH

Some people possess a blessed gift
That must be heaven sent:
They can make a treasured occasion
Of even the simplest event.

SPARED DISILLUSION

Understanding and tolerance
Are ours when we recall
Others are just human, too,
And failings plague us all.

OUTGROWTH

A generous hand is
the extension of a grateful heart.

BONDING AGENT

The castle of life you build
is only as strong as the mortar of integrity
that holds it together.

RECIPROCITY

Success works for you—
after you've worked for it!

PERSONAL INVENTORY

We constantly "take stock" of those about us. We observe
how attractively the "merchandise" is packaged and displayed,
and how effectively it is being marketed.
But how often do we turn
"inventory-eyes" on ourselves?

WIND AND BRASS

We should be sure our tune is worth playing
before we start tooting our own horn!

ON RECORD

A man's word is only as valuable
as the promises he has fulfilled.

RECESS

Relief from one's own worries
May at times be brought
By concentrating less on self
And giving others thought.

PALATABLE PALAVER

Our words are best kept soft and sweet
because we may have to eat them!

MIND OVER MATTER

A drop of deliberate thought
may save a bucket of sweat.

S. O. S.

To deserve the helping hand of an ally,
one must put up a good fight himself!

IN RETROSPECT

The frustrating hindrance
that caused us disappointment today
may be recognized as a blessing in disguise
when reviewed tomorrow.

A WILL TO WIN

Resourceful is the man
Who uses life's chains
For teething rings
And its bonds
For jumping ropes.

FINAL INSTALLMENT

This "waiting for tomorrow"
To enjoy what's hoped for then
Can be a long-continued story . . .
And we may miss the end!

THE DRIVER'S SEAT

Emotions must not have control
When attempting to reach a goal.
Efforts to succeed, instead,
Are best directed by the head.

LESS WEIGHTY

Listening to another fellow's problems
may actually help to lighten one's own.

LOCKED JAWS

One can often avoid being caught in a trap
just by keeping his own shut!

ALONG THE WAY

The road one travels is often
more rewarding and interesting
than the destination itself.

DISTILLED ESSENCE

Whether the perfume
of tomorrow's memories
will be pleasant and sweet
depends upon the ingredients
we pluck from Life's garden today.

THE APPRAISAL

A cause cannot always be rightly judged
by the man who supports it,
but a man can usually be fairly measured
by the causes he supports.

AS WE SOW

We often grow most ourselves
when fostering growth in others.

THE AFTER-TASTE

The tongue that voices kind thoughts
spares itself the bite of bitter remorse.

COMBINED EFFORT

A man who appreciates a helping hand
responds with more than dead weight!

SPECIAL RESERVE

Though he may have few pennies,
the man with plenty of sense
is never a pauper.

SOLO FOR SAFETY

When you are responsible
For getting it done,
You'd better make yourself
A committee of one!

WEIGHED IN THE BALANCE

The greater the value man places
upon his own time and energies,
the less trivial are the irritations
that can claim his attention.

BETTER SAFE THAN SORRY

With a lamb, you can be a lamb;
with a wolf, you'd better be a fox.

PRIVATE INVESTIGATOR

When a problem arises involving some doubt,
It's not a time to guess—but a time to find out!

BATTLE STRATEGY

One of the surest ways to effect
A seeming enemy's end
Is simply by getting to know him
And making him a friend.

PLANT FERTILE FIELDS

Since we can never teach one
Who has no desire to learn,
Time is best devoted to those
Who won't such efforts spurn.

COMING EVENTS

Don't concede before the final round
has been fought to a decision.
What resembles dark defeat
is often only the shadow
of approaching victory.

SAME SPIGOT, SWEET OR SOUR

Operated by the mind,
The tongue is a strange faucet:
Drips honey, spews venom.
It can smite, it can soothe,
It can praise, it can damn.
And by the outpourings of his tongue
A man's heart can often be judged.

RECOGNIZED EMBLEM

The true hallmark of hospitality
is not so much the open door
as the open heart.

SOMETHING TO THINK ABOUT

Time will tell if you've become
An ancestor claimed with pride,
Or a skeleton in the family closet
That your descendants seek to hide!

TURNING POINT

A stumbling block can be a milestone—
if it jolts us onto the right track.

TAKE A CLOSER LOOK

What appears to be "greener pastures"
may be nothing but a patch of weeds!

DUAL RESPONSIBILITY

Enjoying another's confidence
imposes a double duty—
to prove one's own competence
and the other's good judgment!

DIAGNOSIS

Are things just not going right?
Nerves shattered, tensions tight?
Others at fault? That may be true;
But could it be, at least partly, you?
Examine yourself, and then look about,
Discover the cause and put it to rout.
Perhaps when self has been rearranged,
You'll discover all has happily changed.

PRODIGAL, BEWARE

Lose a dime, toss away a dollar—
More can usually be obtained.
But a wasted hour or misspent day
Cannot ever be regained.

CINDERELLA'S SLIPPER

Trying to fill another's shoes
Is rarely ever a cinch.
If too big, they flop about,
And if too small, they pinch!

WAND OR CLUB

The same dollar can harm or aid, work good or ill.
Like a genie in a bewitched bottle, it obeys its master.
Possessors of money exercise powerful green magic:
Their use can make it a golden wand or a glittering club!

MAIN ATTRACTION

The beauty of the canary's plumage is noted,
but the bird will be valued for its song.

BEAUTY DISARMS

We cautiously avoid the thorns on a cactus
but may become careless when handling a rose!

THE PIONEER SPIRIT

By daring to try new roads,
Man shortens distances
And lightens his loads!

TINDERBOX

Emotion only adds fuel to a fire,
but common sense can bank it.

WANT TO BE AN "ANGEL"?

When those we might expect to do so
fail to seek our counsel and advice,
we may feel hurt.
Perhaps we're lucky!
People who insist on getting into the act
often end up having to back the show!

LAME-BRAIN

Some will claim ignorance is bliss;
But who enjoys mental paralysis?

SOAP BUBBLES

Friendships too hastily made
Often just as quickly fade!

PROFIT OR LOSS

While the fruit of discussion is often gain,
The result of argument is usually pain.

LOSS OF TRACTION

Like a tire trapped by ice or mud,
when emotion robs us of our grip
we whirl and spin, burn ourselves up,
wear ourselves out—but get nowhere!

WHIPPING BOY

Those most rebellious
at being "pushed around"
are often unaware
that they themselves
are wielding the whip.

FOWL-PLAY

A wise owl becomes a silly goose
When he lets his tongue get too loose!

A SUGARY SNARE

Though the syrup of flattery is sweet,
it can become a glue that entraps.

SENSE OF VALUES

Often those who insist
on getting their money's worth
shortchange themselves
in spending their time.

IMPOTENT CHARMS

While a man idly waits
for Fortune to seek him out,
his good-luck horseshoe rusts,
and his four-leaf clover wilts.

FOOD FOR THOUGHT

If man allows his own interests
to become all-consuming,
he himself may be devoured!

OWN WORST ENEMY

The first step to self-defeat
Is the practice of self-deceit!

FITTED—BUT FIT?

Another may furnish the saddle,
the bridle—even the horse.
But once you're mounted up,
you're on your own!

TIME TO SPEAK UP

Since silence is often taken for assent,
personal integrity demands we protest
those positive assertions
with which we do not agree
if we're to retain our self-respect.

FORGE AHEAD

The iron in the fire of action grows hotter
than any kept in the ashes of regret.

INNER CORROSION

One's heart and mind fall victims to attrition
When gnawed by devils of doubt and suspicion.

MENTAL MAGIC

Some rely on talismans and charms
Or a rabbit's foot for success:
Wiser heads aim for achievement
Through their own resourcefulness.

ALERTNESS NEEDED

Opportunity often travels disguised.
Many let it slip by—unrecognized!

BLAMING THE BUCK

Money is often referred to as evil.
But any evil attached to money lies
in the means by which some obtain it
and in the ways some misuse it.

TRADED FOR A HUNCH

One is foolish to disregard
his five natural senses
to rely on a so-called "sixth"!

CULINARY FAILURE

Poor judgment and overconfidence
Are ingredients for incompetence.

PACE-SETTER

Unless a man has
consideration for his own time,
others are not likely to do so.

STATUS QUO?

Most of us have asked at some time,
"Why does everything happen to me?"
But how many of us would risk
trading places with another?

COMMON ILLNESS

Discontent is the penalty we pay
for being ungrateful for what we have.

THE STIMULUS

Just as it takes irritation
for the oyster to produce a pearl,
some people require a little "needling"
to accomplish a goal.

COMMON GROUND

Thank goodness everyone can make a mistake.
Human fallibility is a great leveler!

HORSE SENSE

Some find it easier to attract and hold
the interest and attention of others
by remembering how the horse is kept moving
by carrots dangled within sight
but just out of reach.

RETURN ENGAGEMENT

Wishing a problem away
is like locking a ghost in a closet.
You can be sure
it will continue to haunt you.

EXCESS BAGGAGE

Some people with potential
for soaring to great heights
so burden themselves
with trivial details
they can't get off the ground!

THE ESCAPIST

He deprives and endangers himself
who makes retreat from reality
a constant condition.
Closed eyes, ears and minds
shut out many of the riches of life
and make one vulnerable to surprise attack.

PRICE OF GREED

Sometimes one who has sufficient
to be comfortable and content
foolishly risks it to get more
and so turns life's golden cup of plenty
into an empty one of rusty tin!

DEAD ISSUES

When unpleasant things are over and done,
And there's nothing more that you can do,
Don't let them gnaw your brain and heart—
Let them be past, let them be through!

PETTICOAT POWER

A woman's intuition
often triumphs over
a man's reason.
Otherwise there'd be
more bachelors!

NEEDED: A TIGER SWATTER

On petty and trivial annoyances
we often waste mental and physical energies
that may be sorely needed
in moments of real crisis.
We become so exhausted from swatting at flies
we're left helpless when confronted by a tiger!

KNOW YOUR PATIENT

One for whom we too hastily provide crutches
may never again try to walk without them!

WITHOUT LIMITS

Man is the center of his own universe.
Its boundaries can become as great
and its horizons as wide as he allows.

MARCHING WITH TIME

Failure to adjust
as times continue to change
leaves us on the sidelines—
or puts us out of step
in life's big parade!

NO PROXY

Success has always been an elusive prey
for those depending on others
to pave their way!

YOUR OWN HOST

Why always save the best for guests?
Treat yourself like company once in a while.

OWNER OR OWNED?

One who lets possessions
become obsessions
ceases to be master!

THE PANIC BUTTON

Just because you can't take it with you,
you don't have to kill yourself living it up!

IN THE CLINCHES

There are those who talk a great fight
but never throw a punch in the ring.

MAKE YOUR DREAMS COME TRUE

Something special you want to do?
A particular place you want to go?
How long are you going to wait?
Till you lose your money and can't afford it?
Till your health declines so you dare not risk it?
Till you grow too old to fully enjoy it?
What are you waiting for?

MISNOMER

There is nothing *big* in bigotry!

TROJAN PONY

He runs the risk of finding false teeth
who looks a gift horse in the mouth.

UNBALANCED DIET

Many suffer a peculiar malnutrition:
they're overfed with criticism
and starved for a little praise.

SWEET MUSIC

Saying things another wants to hear
Guarantees that person's receptive ear.

NOTHING GAINED

Your emotions have felt the wringer,
You've been in many a stew.
You've fretted and fussed and fumed,
And what's it accomplished for you?

MESS OF POTTAGE

Some grab at little luxuries
Which they can ill afford,
Scorning today's self-denial
That secures tomorrow's reward.

POWERFUL PASTE

Often when one sinks into a rocking chair
Some strange glue will hold him there.

HARD TO GET, HARDER TO LOSE

Some things we are so eager to acquire
we become even more anxious to discard.

STAND TALL

Don't sell yourself short.
You can leave that to others!

UNLUCKY?

"Bad luck" is often made
the convenient peg on which
man hangs what is really
his own incompetence.

SMOKE SCREEN

Not all hustle and bustle
signifies enterprise.
At times a flurry of activity
is intended to obscure
lack of ability.

PERSONAL ACCOUNTING

Most people will attribute their failures
to anything except their own deficiencies.

DOUBLE FEATURE

One's efforts to cause another's loss of face
are rarely without risk to his own!

KNIFE SLIPS

We sometimes
let our tongues
cut our own throats!

KEEP IN TRAINING

When a race has been lost,
It is over and done;
But there remain others
To be run and won.

AROUND THE BUSH

When instead of a simple statement
You get a verbal stew,
Maybe alibis and justifications
Are being served to you.

TRY WORK

Only a hare can reach his goal on a rabbit's foot.

EVIL TWINS

The open mouth and the closed mind
make a most treacherous pair.

ATTITUDE FOR FAILURE

There is no job so small
that it can't defeat the man
who thinks he's too big for it!

IF AT FIRST . . .

If we let discouragement convince us
That we are licked, we're through.
But sheer persistence may reveal
Something more that we can do.
From some failures experience gained
Teaches what to avoid so goals are attained.

GOING SOMEWHERE?

You may "put your best foot forward,"
but unless you follow through with the other,
how far will you get?

TRIBUTE

Age alone may command courtesy;
Money can often buy it.
Honors may be purchased, too.
But respect is earned or won
Through one's thoughts and deeds.

A MATTER OF GRAVITY

One can coast only so long
before coming to a dead stop
—unless he's going downhill!

EVALUATIONS

How desperate a man's need
or how demanding his desire
may determine the value
he places on anything.
A drop of water, or a crust of bread,
when it might preserve life itself,
becomes the most precious thing
in the world.

WORD IS BOND

Since a promise exposes one's integrity
To others' most scrutinizing view,
Tongue or pen should be restrained
If there's no intent to follow through.

NOTE TO HAND-WRINGERS

If we quickly effected their repair,
Some of our troubles wouldn't breed despair.

THAWING FROZEN ASSETS

Trying to bring out of people
qualities and abilities not in them
is "priming a dry well."
Only in helping them to discover
and develop those they do have
is there likelihood of success.

MASTER OF ARTIFICE

Beware of conjecture:
It can produce hopes and fears—
and both may be false!

IN EVIDENCE

Before you give people
credit for common sense,
be sure they're using it.

SNAP-TRAPS

Snap judgments often snap back!

APPLICATION

By planning our work
and working our plans,
We gather more honey—
and keep out of jams!

CHOPPING BLOCK

There are always those who have an axe to grind.
The grinding noise may annoy, but our real concern
should be where and when the sharpened edge will fall.
Not even a chicken drapes its own neck under the blade.

REDEEMABLE, BUT . . .

It's never easy to buy yourself back
once you've sold yourself out!

POINTED PRESSURE

A prodding pitchfork produces action,
but it rarely stimulates cooperation.

FORERUNNER

To stay out in front
one must have more
than just front!

SPECIAL ENVOY

You're represented by your gift;
Make this your guiding cue:
Presents selected with thought and care
Are those that do credit to you.

SNUG BUG

A man may grow complacent
and feel "snug as a bug in a rug."
But if he's smart, he keeps
a weather-eye peeled to avoid
being taken to the cleaners.

TIGHTENING GRIP

A vice may become a vise,
squeezing one into slavery.

OVERTURE

You can't shake hands
with a clenched fist.

BEDFELLOWS

Covering up for another often involves
exposing ourselves!

BAD COMPANIONS

Instead of treating irritations
as casual passers-by,
some insist on making
bosom-buddies of them!

PART II

Living and Growing

TO OR FOR ANOTHER

Be it a helping hand, a kind word or a smile,
giving of one's self promotes the sense
of a worthwhile reason for being.

SOLID FOUNDATION

For cornerstones on which to build
the wise never choose the "rolling kind."

THE HOMING VARIETY

We pamper and coddle some of our troubles
until they become pet pigeons
returning regularly to the same old roost.
Forced out of the nest while yet fledglings,
many will fly away for good.

FOR THEIR OWN GOOD

True love often is best expressed
by denying another's foolish whim
or harmful desire.

FALSE PROMISE

Many a road that lures us
turns out to be a dead-end street.

THE TEST

You can lift your fellow man to his feet,
but the test of his interest and character
is whether he endeavors to walk on his own.

THE "FREE" BAIT

"Something for nothing" has its lure,
even though it often costs
more than it's worth!

WHAT SHALL IT PROFIT?

From lowly beginnings through effort, stress and strain,
He climbed to a position of importance and fame.
Now, the diagnosis, which his doctor has explained,
Shows he paid too great a price for what he has gained.

STATE OF SERENITY

Wise is the man who, having achieved peace of mind,
is able to resist those things that could destroy it.

FAMILIAR BRUISES

Many have suffered contusions
From jumping to conclusions!

ONLY TEMPORARY

Defeat does not always mean surrender.
One may bow to superior strength
without abandoning his point of view
or hope of victory in the next encounter.

PENALIZING SELF

Allowing others' inconsiderate ways
To upset us to distraction,
We suffer first the hurt itself—
And then from our own reaction.

QUESTIONABLE LUXURY

Indifference to the world about us
can only be afforded
by those who've left it.

BETTER RETURNS

A generous man enjoys more comfort from little
than the miser extracts from much.

STAMP OF VALIDITY

Pride of possessions is justified
by the worthwhile use made of them.

MENTAL FEATS

There are times when forgetting
can be just as important as remembering
—and even more difficult!

EARTH-BOUND

Each night of your life
You may wish on a star...
But a century of wishing
Leaves you just where you are.

APPRECIATION'S RESPONSE

To the artist, it's enthusiastic applause;
To the giver, it's a sincere "thank you."
In effect they are one and the same—
Expressions enriching and ennobling acts.

SAUCE FOR THE GOOSE

Why do we expect others to change
and so resist change ourselves?

RETIREMENT'S URGE

The man who's always been active
May find it hard to just recline.
So he'll look for a task or purpose
That merits his effort and time.

This search may grow rather frantic,
And he might get in your hair;
But be patient and try to see his plight,
For one day you, too, will be there.

THE HEROES

Be it the bravery of a moment's deed
Or daily courage of a lifetime's need,
Each is entitled to respect and reward.

BRIDLE FOR BEGINNERS

We make success more likely
for the inexperienced person
to whom we give new opportunity
by "giving him his head"—while
keeping a gentle "bit" in his mouth
and a watchful hand on the "rein."

BLADE OF FATE

Were we conscious of the sword
Held o'erhead by a single hair,
Like Damocles, we'd speak and move
With greater gentleness and care.

MEMORY TRIUMPHS

The laurel wreath is withered,
But I recall it on my brow.
Fortune's smiles are so long absent,
I'm called a "has-been" now.
But the memory of triumphs
That drew my peers' acclaim
Inspires me to pity those
Who have never tasted fame.

A HARD LESSON

Often there is more virtue
and more reward
in learning to like what you must do
than to insist on doing what you like.

SHARED LAUGHTER

Going through life I have learned
A sense of humor begins at home.
When with cause someone laughs at me,
He does not laugh alone.

THE SILVER LINING

Something good can come from most situations,
even if it is only learning to avoid similar ones.

SKIN-DEEP

A blemished skin does not mean
the apple won't make a fine pie!

NO CAUSE FOR WORRY

"Will you still love me," she asked,
"When I've grown old and gray?"
"Don't worry, Pet," he assured,
"Beauty shops are here to stay."

SOLELY RESPONSIBLE

When we choose how we will live,
we become weavers at looms of our own,
working the texture and pattern of our lives.
We cannot disown or shift to another
responsibility for our design.

YOU FIND WHAT YOU SEEK

One intent on finding the good in others
encounters fewer faults.

SPARED BY SERVICE

'Tis a curious thing and one worth noting:
Those concerned with the welfare of others
seem to have fewer problems of their own.

QUESTION FOR THE GIRLS

In most men there's some Huck Finn
And a little dash of Fauntleroy.
Is that what makes him lovable, girls—
This reflection of the boy?

SPILT MILK

Don't bemoan what might have been;
Destiny often takes peculiar quirks.
Instead of better, as you suppose,
Things might have been even worse!

ON FATHER'S DAY

Whether we call him Pop
Or refer to him as Dad,
Our own father seems to us
The best anyone ever had.

Though on this day set aside for him
Some special honors he may accrue,
Most treasured is the love and respect
Which we show him all year through.

ON THE HOME FRONT

An additional value of *our* vacation
is the rest it provides for others.

VACANCY CREATED

The best way to move into your superior's job
is to support his efforts to get a better one.

MAZE OF MAKE-BELIEVE

It's so easy to believe
what we want to believe
that truth often gets lost
behind the veil of self-delusion.

UNBIASED RECOGNITION

He is a friend
who gives honest praise to our virtues
and understanding to our shortcomings.

LASTING GLOW

Of things making life worthwhile
Few can ever quite match
A friend's warm, understanding heart
With its door left off the latch.

WAKE UP AND LIVE

Although we can be certain of change,
we never know in what direction.
Remaining conscious
of this imponderable of life
urges our use and enjoyment
of more of what we have
while we are able.

ORAL CAMOUFLAGE

There are those who whistle to hide their fears,
And many who sing to hold back their tears.

ACCORDING TO HOYLE

In life, as in any game,
There are rules controlling play.
For each breach or careless move
There's a penalty to pay.

When a foot gets heavy on the gas,
A traffic ticket applies a "brake";
And for wrong food or too much,
The "fine" is often a stomach-ache.

A FORK IN THE ROAD

The person who really wants to do something
finds a way, while others look for an excuse!

FASHION PLATE

They wear their years most becomingly
who have remained young in heart
while managing to grow up!

TO THE RESCUE

Tension-charged atmosphere can be relieved
and threatened situations can often be saved
by one wise enough to mask his inner feelings.

MATTER OF JUDGMENT

He who places confidence in everyone
may become a pauper,
but he who places confidence in no one
is already destitute.

DISCRETION

Sometimes it takes
"more of a man"
to seem a "mouse."

HEART BALM

Although love is wonderful professed,
It's much more comforting possessed.

JUST BETWEEN US

Our friends are really aging,
Don't you agree?
I wonder if they're envious
When they look at you and me?

EACH DAY ITS OWN

By leaving yesterday's troubles to the past
and tomorrow's to the future,
we are better able to take care of today's
and to enjoy some pleasure along the way.

CROSS FIRE

The peacemaker between
embattled husband and wife
is often the only casualty!

POINT OF VIEW

Foresight acts to shape history;
hindsight may only read it!

TO THE POINT

Why live for today only?
It will be past tomorrow.

CITY FARMER

Hurry and worry
are fertilizers
for raising ulcers!

THE PAY-OFF

Each of us has abilities
In differing amounts;
It's not the capabilities,
But how they're used, that counts!

THE "ESTATE" WE BUILD

Today we inherit the benefits earned yesterday.
Tomorrow we'll be heir to what we do today.

TOTAL ERROR

We've heard it said we're entitled
To at least one mistake.
It's certain if the first is fatal,
We won't a second make!

HAPPY TEARS

Many men who bear pain without a tear
sometimes are moved to weep for joy.

WARPED VALUES

'Tis a curious irony
that many who are misers with dollars
are such spendthrifts with their time.
Ironical, too,
that all the dollars they've hoarded
can't redeem the hours squandered.

DEMAND AND DRIVE

On yesterday's laurels one cannot rest;
Today's must, too, be earned.
For by the world that cheered us yesterday,
Today we may be spurned.

THE HITCHHIKER

Running away from yourself
is never a solo flight.
What you seek to escape
always rides piggy-back!

PLEASURE DEFERRED

A shock brings some to realize,
Often with sorrow and regret,
That they put off unnecessarily
Things they meant to do or get.
They kept postponing until too late
And now, deprived, blame all on fate.

LISTENER POLL

A man's conduct indicates
the strength of his conscience
and how well he listens to its voice.

OTHERS FLIRT WITH FAILURE

In life's race the winners are those
who refuse to allow fleeting whims
to divert their attention and efforts
from the goal line!

SCARLESS

The malicious thought never put into words
is like the arrow never loosed from the bow.
Neither wounds.

DEEPER THAN TASTE

To one who has suffered indigestion,
the "proof of the pudding"
is not merely in the eating!

WHERE'S THE EVIDENCE?

One's boast that he's never had a failure
is no proof that he's a success!

TREACHEROUS GAL

Although a tempting dish,
Lady Luck is fickle
and not to be trusted.
She often drops her title
to be plain Miss Fortune!

A THING REFLECTED

Why expect concern from others
When we're displaying none?
It is only when we care enough
That another's interest is won.

THE FILLED NEED

One who has known hunger
best appreciates the loaf of bread.

STORMY SESSION

When emotion gets so loud that reason can't be heard,
Discussion ends and argument becomes the word!

INVITATION TO DISASTER

Collecting antiques can be a profitable hobby;
clinging to antiquated ideas can be costly folly.

THE WEALTH OF LOVE

The infant craves love; the child yearns for it;
all through one's years the hunger is ever there.
Although he be cloaked in gold and power,
until this great need is fulfilled,
no man is truly rich!

TEAMMATES

Working without a plan
is not quite so useless
as planning without work.

ROUGH DRAFT

Thoughts committed to paper can be erased;
spoken into another's ear, they're past recall.

FAR LESS PAINFUL

Why create troubles of our own
when others will so willingly
share theirs?

BLINDFOLDED?

People who keep saying, "Things don't change much,"
are probably looking in yesterday's mirror.

SIGN LANGUAGE

Affection spoken only in words
May like the real thing appear,
But love's silent language is told
In gestures only the soul can hear.

CALENDAR-GAUGE

Age, an accepted guide
to the quality of a wine,
is an unreliable yardstick
for measuring maturity of man.

TUNE AND TEMPO

A song in your heart puts a spring in your walk,
Brings a smile to your lips and a sparkle to your talk
—But not when you're singing the blues!

BE PREPARED

When too many of our problems
By other hands are eased,
In time by some strange weakness
We find our spirits seized.

Best to keep our mental muscles
In practice and in tone,
So that when the need arises
We can do the job alone.

OVERCONCILIATORY

A person can be broken
by too frequently
bending over backwards
to please others!

AN UPSTREAM PULL

Eventually man finds
he has to paddle his own canoe.
Others are too busy
propelling theirs!

COMPLETELY LOST

No one interest should be
all things to a person,
absorbing him completely.
For if that one thing be taken away
it leaves his whole world shattered.

EXTERMINATOR NEEDED

Like termites,
trivial annoyances
and petty aggravations
gnaw away at your brain.
The one
makes sawdust of timbers,
the other of your head!

CRACKED "CHESTNUT"

The old adage declares,
"Absence makes the heart grow fonder."
But history shows
unoccupied thrones are often usurped!

ENVIRONMENTAL BIAS

Regardless how objective we may claim to be,
personal background influences our viewpoints.
What is "principle" to one
may be "prejudice" to another.

THE GREATER LOSS

Without realizing it, when you let another down,
You may let yourself down even more.
The victim may recover from hurt feelings,
but lost esteem and confidence are rarely regained.

WARNING WHISPER

A hollow voice hissed in his ear,
"What's your rush? I'll wait for you."
Recognizing the hovering Shadow,
the speeder lost any desire to hurry.

PROMISES, PROMISES

Words without action
are hollow sounds
just beating on the eardrums,
never touching the heartstrings!

TALLY SHEET

Like baseball players,
we prefer to hear about
our "hits" and "runs"
rather than our "errors."

TAKES MORE THAN TEARS

It is a natural thing to weep,
And it sometimes brings relief.
But tears alone won't wash away
Or overcome the cause of grief.

FOOTING THE BILL

Those who feel they are learning
at their own expense
often fail to recognize
what it may be costing others.

WITH EYES WIDE OPEN

Recognizing that there are
various types of "friends,"
and that each in his own way
contributes different values
to our lives may spare us disillusion.

WILLINGNESS TO ACCEPT

One's opinions are best kept flexible
and his conclusions only temporary.
    For what today is accepted as fact
    tomorrow may be exploded
    as fancy, fiction or fallacy!

BARBED BLADE

No weapon
can wound more deeply
than the human tongue.

RIPPLING RHYTHM

Some are like the babbling brook,
Always pleasant to hear;
Although often it is only chatter,
It's music to the ear.

LAST, BUT NOT LEAST

Both the tail of the kite
and the train's caboose
serve useful purposes.

UNIVERSAL SOCIETY

The man who makes a mistake
reaffirms his membership
in the world's oldest fraternity.

APOLOGY IN ACTION

Regrets for errors or oversights
Are little help to anyone.
Constructive amends are those
That see things properly done.

WARNING TO "PYGMALIONS"

Attempts to make another person over
frequently result in change to one's self.

PARADOX

The most reckless people
may well be those
who never take a chance!

MEMORY'S RICHES

The laurel leaf is tender,
Only briefly does it last;
But he whose brow
The wreath adorned
In memory holds it fast.

THE SURRENDER

Some have been known
to extend recuperation
into a lifetime vacation.

THE REVIEWING STAND

Let us reflect at the end of day
On things we've thought and done,
Checking if they were truly worthwhile—
For ourselves or for anyone.

PART III

Calling a Spade a Spade

PERPETUAL DISCONTENT

For the "insatiables"
sufficient never seems enough;
enough never seems sufficient.

CHANGED CURRICULUM

Reading, 'riting and 'rithmetic—
Those dear old 3-R's—seem dead.
It's Riot, Release and Rebellion
Many students now follow instead!

VOICE OF ENVY

The success one has earned
By preparedness and pluck
Will be envied by many
Who will call it "just luck."

ESCAPE HATCH

Some people are not so dumb
as they'd lead others to believe.
It's their way of making sure
no one expects too much of them.

"CONS" AND "PROS"

Beggars can't be choosers,
but they can be critics!

NO WET BLANKETS

To keep the atmosphere happy,
One soon learns to shun
Those who are always griping
And spoiling others' fun.

TEMPUS FUGIT

Those who live in the past
often complain about the present
and express little hope for the future.

BEHIND THE MASK

Pretended concern
often disguises
selfish curiosity!

VERBAL ASSASSINATION

An enemy, with his words,
may forge a sword as deadly
as any made by an armorer.
The one may take your life;
the other destroys your name
and rips away your honor!

THE FIREBUG

The words or acts may have been willful
That had so aroused his ire,
Or may have been done unconsciously . . .
But they kindled quite a fire.
The one to whom the match was set,
By his anger was burned to a cinder;
While the one who had lighted the fuse
Went his way with nought to hinder!

CAST YOUR BREAD . . .

You're foolish to wait
for your ship to come in,
if you haven't bothered
to send one out!

FIGHTING STANCE

One doesn't always have to keep
his backbone arched
to prove he has one!

THE DEBTOR

"I will always be indebted to you," he said.
And he was—for he made no effort to repay.

TOO QUICK ON THE DRAW?

Fame, you wandering hunter,
How do you pick your game?
I've examined some specimens:
At times you take poor aim!

BOGUS BOND

People whose word is worthless
have devalued it themselves!

YOUTH'S FOLLY

At both ends he burned the candle,
Living riotously, fast and bold.
When self-realization finally came,
His excesses had made him old!

SOMEONE ELSE'S NECK

Some are always willing
to stick another's neck out
—and to take the credit
if the risk pays off!

SOAPBOX STAMPEDE

If enough noise is stirred up on any issue,
many will join the howling pack,
ignorant as to the worth of the cause!

LOUD AND CLEAR

It's surprising how deaf
Some people can be
Except to the jingle of coin
Or the rustle of currency!

POT AND KETTLE

Those who laugh at others' faults
too often lack the good sense
to examine themselves for flaws.

SHORT MEMORY

He scarcely deserves the rewards of success
who is no longer grateful or gracious enough
to remember those who helped him get his start!

ADDED LINKS

Alibis and lame excuses
only serve to lengthen
one's chain of abuses!

NARROW ORBIT

For the one who thinks of self alone,
The fields are few his mind to roam.

"TOP DOG"

Some are not particular what kind of heap it is,
so long as they can be on top of it!

ONLY WHEN NEEDED

If I am denied the pleasure
of sharing your joys,
kindly spare me the pain
of wrestling with your problems.

THE SILENT SABOTEUR

Intentionally withholding facts that
in fairness should be disclosed
is a deception as treacherous
as telling a deliberate lie!

PRICE-TAG CONSCIOUS

Instead of getting joy and a lift,
Some sharply appraise every gift.
They wonder why it is not more—
Or didn't come from a classier store!

RENEGING

Some who are quickest to promise help
are slowest to extend it!

BOARDINGHOUSE REACH

A greedy grab invites a painful stab!

SHORT CUT TO SOCIAL EXILE

Public belittling of one's spouse
May keep a bully's own ego fat;
But such acts disgust spectators,
Who soon leave such tyrants flat!

THOUGHT ON HALLOWE'EN

This is the gremlins' and goblins' night to howl,
But we need have no fear—
They are no more frightening on their prowl
Than some we meet all year!

PURSUIT OF HAPPINESS

The constitutional guarantee
of the pursuit of happiness
is misinterpreted by some
as license to trample anyone
who gets in their way.

CANINE COMEUPPANCE

The dog so stupid or unappreciative
as to bite the hand that feeds him
may come to know hunger!

THE INTOXICANTS

Success or wine, when they go to his head,
can make one unpleasant company.

FACT OF THE MATTER

"I would if I could,"
Some always sigh.
They could if they would;
Why don't they try?

SPENDTHRIFTS

Some who are always giving
others a piece of their minds
can ill afford it!

TOUCH OF FEVER

It is regrettable that
the degree of honesty in some
is relative to their need
or determined by their greed.

POST-HOLIDAY SLUMP

The consideration some start showing
just before Christmas often starts
wearing off soon after New Year's.

COVER-UP

Sometimes a veneer of indifference
masks a hollow shell of ignorance.

SUDDEN STOPPER

Those criticizing others
for things they also have done
may be embarrassed
by skeletons of their past
rattled by a knowing one!

WHEN THE FUR FLIES

Many a sly fox has been caught
in a trap of his own devising!

UP FRONT!

He who will clamor and fight
Always to be first
May find when things get tight
That spot's the worst!

BEARS IN A BULL MARKET

Persons of ability who limit their performance
to meet only the minimum requirements of a job
sell themselves short.

TIME-THIEF

When we waste another's time,
we take from him that
which we cannot replace.

STRINGS ATTACHED

One who regards the recipient
of his favors or helpful acts
as his "debtor" is not a giver.
He's a "mortgage-holder,"
and his acts are deals, not deeds!

STRAIN-BRAINS

Some brains are like sieves;
they retain only the chaff.

ALTERNATIVE

One who chooses not to use his brain
had better have a strong back
or rich relatives and friends!

BELATED TRUCE

When the vindictive spirit of a few
carries family squabbles on and on,
natural relationships are lost to many.
Reasonably reconciled differences
could mend breached family ties,
yet some wait to "bury the hatchet"
at some innocent's final resting place.

GROUNDS FOR SUSPICION

Because his sympathy for others
Was just hollow words, unfelt,
He could only wonder how sincere
Was that he received himself.

A TOUCHY SUBJECT

Some are never in touch—except for a touch!

HARD TO SWALLOW

A person may "sugar-coat" his conscience
until it becomes a bitter pill to others!

VANITY FAIR

Expensive couture and fancy coiffure
Often result in new hauteur!

DELINQUENT DABBLERS

While some parents do pastime painting
    Or modeling in clay,
Their children often go "arty" in
    A much more primitive way.
Frequently they paint the town blood-red;
    With "sculpture," too, they putter:
Instead of clay, they use their knives
    To simply carve each other!
If parents and kids spent more time
    Together in work and play,
Their lives would be molded differently
    And be happier today!

PARK-BENCH PROFESSOR

The man with nothing to do
can usually be found
encouraging others in the art.

MISTAKEN IDENTITY

Some, given the scepter of responsibility,
confuse it with the club of authority.

TESTED

Those who put the "squeeze" on others
usually squeal loudest
when caught in the wringer!

SINGLE-ENTRY LEDGER

Some people easily forget
the dollars you spent on them;
but they always remember
the nickel they lent you!

TIMELY CORRECTION

Some "cute ways" which we indulge
in the spoiled or precocious child
develop into the eccentricities
so scorned in adults.

ACCESSORY

You're not innocent
if you place temptation in the path
of one whose weakness you know
or seek to exploit.

FAMILIARITY BREEDS...

He's a "hale fellow, well met";
But that's close enough to get!

PUSH OR PULL

You never have to ask for a shove down the hill,
but you may have to search for a hand back up!

THE EXTREMISTS

The man who believes everything should be given him
may be stupid;
but he who believes that one can live without help
is no wiser.

LET'S FACE IT!

Sometimes it's not that you are you,
Nor your position that is the bait—
It's what you have that they can get
That serves to make you rate!

THE JUDAS TOUCH

All that which makes a man a man
is cheaply valued by one
who barters friendship for personal gain.

TO DO A JOB

A windbag
is no substitute
for a windmill!

GLORY-GRABBERS

Some who are unwilling to do the work
are always ready to share the credit.

THE FISHING TACKLE

The "angler" tosses out his "line,"
"lures" the prey to take the "bait"—
and another poor "fish" is "hooked"!

DIALECTIC GEOMETRICS

Beware of people who talk in circles.
Often they are not on-the-square!

FULL MEASURE

If a person gives the best
of which he is capable,
it is unfair to expect more
—and unjust to get sore.

ON THE CUFF

Some people are so "cheap"
that others can ill afford
their company!

IN EXILE

He risks the joys of a warm household
For a drafty doghouse out in the cold
Who lets his tongue get so rash and bold
As his mate's kin to attack and scold!

ON DISPLAY

To deny love and respect
where they are due
advertises one's
envy or ingratitude.

FRIGID ROMANCE

The miser nightly caressed his ingots of gold,
Receiving in turn only their touch—hard and cold!

PAUSE THAT IMPRESSES

Each day cuts one's time shorter,
And soon it is too late
To do the things you long to do—
So why procrastinate?

HAGGLE HOBBY

Some take such perverse pleasure in complaining
they reject any reasonable adjustment that
weakens their grounds for griping!

SELECTIVE HEARING

We may be deaf to many sounds,
but always seem to hear
the voice of temptation.

PUPPET TALK

When money talks,
its master is speaking.

FICTION FIXATION

The past some brag about
is the one they've imagined
and have come to believe.

OLD SCRATCH

The devil may offer big wages—
but there's no social security!

NO, THANK YOU!

Although well-intentioned,
it is a dubious compliment
to be called "wise as an owl."
He's blind in the daylight,
preys about in the dark
and hoots all night.
If that's wisdom, who wants it?

CAUSE FOR "SPEC"-ULATION

I bought him glasses so that he might see;
Strange that now he fails to recognize me!

OPTICAL DELUSION

Some use the same magnifying glass
for viewing others' faults
and their own virtues!

THE BEASTS OF BURDEN

The camel, the ox and the mule
one can relieve of their loads;
but man won't let go.

SMOOTH OPERATOR

The smart "milker"
neither tries to take too much
nor goes about it too roughly!

CONTINUOUS CONTEST

Keeping up with the Joneses
is a ruinous hobby.
Neighbor matches neighbor,
folly for folly!

INEQUITY

Those people who censure a single misstep by one
while condoning continual escapades of another
further demonstrate their inconsistency.

MAIN COURSE

No wonder steak is so popular at banquets
—so much bull is shot there!

EFFECTIVE MEASURE

Subjecting man to the same treatment
that he is always giving others
may prove the only way to awaken him
to a mending of his ways.

MISDIRECTED ENERGY

Often those convinced a thing can't be done
exert enough effort proving their stand
to have actually accomplished the feat!

SINGLE HARNESS

One may think that by traveling alone
he'll go farther, faster. But he'll
miss many of the joys along the way
that could have been his if shared.

APPETIZERS

Given too much too often,
many are encouraged
to expect more and more!

INTELLIGENCE LIMITED

Some minds are like Pullman berths at noon
—made up and closed!

CAMOUFLAGE

Many acts conceived by self-interest
are committed in the name of "justice."

FAIR-WEATHER FRIENDS

Some who are fun in the sun
Fail to show when there's snow!

PARE-EMPHASIS

When people get to thinking they're too sharp
they often cut themselves out of things.

MATTER OF OMISSION

Often at personal sacrifice, some give
their children advantages they never had.
While boasting of this, they neglect to provide
important ones they did have that are basic
to building happy and worthwhile lives.
Sometimes the crises of adulthood may bring
the offspring to recognize—even to resent—
their lack of preparation to meet them.

THERE'S A DIFFERENCE

Confidence in one's judgment
Is essential to success,
But vain, headstrong arrogance
Leads often to distress.

INCORRIGIBLES

To err is human—
but why must some people
become chronic offenders?

THE CONVINCER

Many a person's viewpoint
has been influenced
by another's pocketbook.

SURPRISE PACKAGE

Appearances may deceive:
Remember that a lot of junk
is sometimes gift-wrapped!

PARTY LINE

To gossip busy ears wide open are thrown,
Respecting no one's privacy but their own!

CORE OF INGRATITUDE

Some who make the least effort to help themselves
are the most critical of assistance they receive.

A FAIRER GAME

When consideration ceases to be a two-way deal,
one may start playing solitaire.

MANY KINDS OF COIN

You can count on being treated fine
—as long as you pay your own way.

SOUNDING BOARD

The hollow shell of a false front
never echoes the ring of truth!

SALT TREATMENT

Some apologies are worse than the original offense.
Instead of healing, they only aggravate the wound.

A LITTLE DIPLOMACY

The winning approach, which some so lack,
Is that which we label usually as "tact."

UNNECESSARY GAMBLE

One takes quite a chance
When he pays in advance!

FOREVER THE CATERPILLAR

Some people live their entire lives in a cocoon.
They stubbornly resist both instinct and reason
that urge them to take wing into a bigger world.

THE CALCULATORS

Those whose every move has ulterior motives
are suspicious of any kindness another does.

ISOLATIONIST

The man who walls his neighbors out
must be content to live in a tomb.

TAPS!

Gabriel often blows his horn—
for careless drivers who don't!

FILLING THAT COUNTS

In people, as in pies,
we expect more than crust.

GALAXY GOSSIP

Do you wonder if conversations
On Venus, Saturn or Mars—
Like ours—are just comparisons
Of operations, aches and scars?

CHECKING ACCOUNTS

When we feel shortchanged,
let's first examine the coin
we're handing out to others!

NOISY NIMRODS

Some people are like blank cartridges:
They make a lot of noise—but never hit the mark!

COOKING WHOSE GOOSE?

Some rob their own nests
by "killing" the goose
before the golden egg is laid.

A CURE

If forced to listen to themselves,
many people would soon talk less!

HARDER TO RECOGNIZE

Because it may throw one off guard,
a half-truth may be at times
more dangerous than a whole lie!

NOT ON THE MAPS

Where do you find the "point of no return"?
Just make a loan—you may have reached it!

HIS NAME IS LEGION

An ingrate can always find time to ask favors,
but is always too busy to say, "Thanks."

A LITTLE "HEEL"-IUM

Pretentiousness is a shiny balloon
inflated by the gas of self-importance.

MEEOW!

"I'm not going to give my age away,"
said the coy matron.
"I'm sure no one would want that!"
purred the young thing.

CLOSE QUARTERS

Surprising how some dainty mouths
can hold such long, busy tongues.

NOT-SO-TASTY DISH

When one has "cooked his own goose,"
he finds few eager to share the "stew."

RAINY-DAY THRIFT

One may grow so concerned
about some future rain
that he'll never enjoy today's sun.

POOR PROSPECTS

Isn't it foolish to expect something of those
who won't even do anything for themselves?

PART IV

With Eyes Wide Open

EGO-LEVELER

We may boast of harnessing solar energy
Until we recall Who made the sun,
And brag about our irrigation systems
While we forget Who made rivers run;
We may proudly assert mastery over the waves
Until reminded Who made the sea.
Now, while we may claim we've got the world by the tail,
Let's remember Who made the world—and you and me!

THE HERE AND THE NOW

It is well to look ahead to distant horizons,
but not so over-intently that we stumble
over problems lying right at our feet.

APATHY TO ATROPHY

Those who fail to defend
what they profess to love
will find, ultimately,
they can neither defend
nor love anything.

TWISTED TALE?

Never "borrow a page" from another's book
Unless you know how his story ends!

SELF-DRIVEN DROP-OUT

Fruits of their efforts some never taste
Because they're no longer around;
They've continued on at so hard a pace
That prematurely they're under ground.

THE MOUND BUILDERS

A disposition that makes
mountains out of molehills
erects barriers between
valleys of human relationships.

SO—WHAT'S YOUR GRIPE?

It's easy to complain
about the frosting on our cake,
except in the presence of one
who doesn't even have bread.

DE-FUN-ITION

"Cooked Goose": Some bird
who got himself into hot water!

ANOTHER'S ANTE

Venturing nothing of their own,
Some will risk the substance—
Even the very lives—of others.

TOWARD HIGHER GROUND

Though man is flawed
and can never attain perfection,
it is also true that our greatest men
have been consistently undaunted
by the inherent human limitations
accepted by those they left behind.

NO CONTEST

Integrity too weak to withstand
a small temptation
falls easy prey to a big one!

OFT-HEARD ALIBI

Parents who burn up their energies and years
While claiming "it's for the children's sake,"
May give those children finally nought but tears—
For flames most often only ashes make!

UNMASKED

The ungrateful
reveal themselves
to be, also,
the unworthy.

ACUTE INDIGESTION

To the victor, it is said, belongs the spoils;
But the triumph itself may be spoiled
Should the conqueror be overcome by his greed.

THAT TENACIOUS TORTOISE

If we lose sight of our goal
By indulging in off-course play,
As did the fabled hare,
We may find that one less gifted,
And less given to delay,
Has already beaten us there.

A BUM KNIGHT

The chronic critic would complain
about "the pea under the mattress"—
even if his usual bed were a park bench.

CONDESCENSION

We can never be an uplifting influence on
those to whom we insist on talking down.

CLIMATE CHANGERS

Despite man's being created
only a little lower than the angels,
the world seems heavily populated
with devils who, at times,
make it a helluva place to live!

WHAT REALLY COUNTS

None can boast of merely having a good brain;
It's how he uses it that brings pride or shame.

A CACTUS-CUSHION

He is richer who lives in modest means honestly acquired,
Than one who possesses great wealth and honors
Purchased at the price of a gnawing conscience.

POSTSCRIPT TO THE PAST

Those who'd abort its facts or ignore its lessons
cheat themselves of history's benefits.

BY ANY OTHER NAME...!

When one invokes the "virtue of patience"
to excuse a timid will or deadened conscience,
his inaction becomes an unpardonable vice!

MENTAL MITE

Many a man's destroyed himself
Through needless sweat and strain
Because he over-used his back
And so under-used his brain.

TAKEN FOR GRANTED

Like the sun, we oft give others light
And brighten up their darkest night,
But some just never seem to care
If our light is or is not there.
But if we'd take it and depart,
Leaving the ingrates in the dark,
Maybe then they'd come to know
Whence they'd had the warmth and glow,
And learn the "thanks" they did not say
Is why we took that light away.

CEREBRAL STARVATION

A craving of our body may force us to eat our fill;
But the feeding of our mind requires an act of will.

ON PULLING UP STAKES

Let us not hastily our bridges burn
And cut off all chances for return.
For someday maybe we will find
We miss all that we left behind,
But can't go back to old home ground
Or bring another to what we've found.

FLOTSAM AND JETSAM

The man who is content
merely to be carried by the tide
cannot justly complain
if he's washed up on alien shores.

PRIMARY REQUISITE

Before he will seek it, accept it, or apply it,
one must recognize and admit his need of help.

IMMOBILIZED

Who'll weakly quail,
Grow wan and pale
For fear he'll fail
Tries not a thing;
Gets not ahead,
Winds up instead
As good as "dead,"
For not venturing.

BY CONTRAST

We never appreciate a bright, clear morning
So much as after a long, dreary rain;
And it's after some time "under the weather,"
We're most grateful for freedom from pain.

CALCULATING RISKS

More important to success
than the courage to be daring
is knowing when to dare, and how.

SWAPS

Often we trade "our kingdom for a horse"
Only to find the steed is either lame or blind.

DELUSION'S DIFFUSION

The rose-colored glasses, through which
some insist on viewing the world,
may seem to brighten life's dark shadows
but they do nothing to eliminate
that which casts them.

FILTHY LUCRE?

The disdain or aversion for money some profess
is to rationalize resentment over lack of it.

AN ACID CALLED REGRET

To brood incessantly
over past losses or mistakes
dissipates one's peace of mind.
For tears shed over split milk,
will sour the mind and heart,
and eventually make all the fruits
of one's life taste bitter.

THEY BITE THE HAND…!

By spurning the giver but not his gift,
By scorning the caretaker but not his care,
By insulting the donor while taking his charity,
Some people, in their own perverse way,
Seek to assert an independence
That they resent is not wholly theirs.

THE GOLDEN APPLE

The seeds of fundamental sincerity yield many fruits,
not the least of which is the trust of one's fellow men.

CRITIQUE

Be not offended, madam,
Though he says your dress
Looks quite a mess;
For without it you may
Have gone on your way
Without ever knowing
Your slip was showing.

ATTITUDE FOR LONELINESS

Because they receive no dividends,
when our interest lies only in self,
others are discouraged from investing
their time and attention in us.

GIFT BY GRIFT

It is not charitable to give one man cake,
If to do so, you've taken another man's bread!

TRAFFIC'S FLOW

The road from our youth
Is like a one-way street:
It admits of no return.
One who tries that path to retrace
Back to seemingly brighter yesterdays
Makes little progress—
But creates a lot of problems
For himself and those about him.

BROAD IS THE WAY...!

"Good intentions," it is said,
"Oft pave the road to hell."
And one can't escape the devil's bed
By saying, "I meant well."

CHECKS AND BALANCES

Extremism in the pursuit of treasure is no virtue;
and moderation in the pursuit of pleasure is no vice!

RECEPTION: A—O.K.

By tuning ourselves out
from any reality of sorrow
we may also weaken or lose
our wavelength to joy.

SUBSIDY FOR SUBSEQUENT SPOUSES

Some overwork themselves to death,
thereby endowing their successors
with all the fruits of their labors.

SPIRITUAL PARALYSIS

When the prospect of personal gain is great
And the fear of penalty is slight,
Temptation seems easily to numb some
To pleas of conscience for moral right.

WASTE NOT, WANT NOT

A gentle shower makes the flowers grow;
A flood may wash all away.
Let that remind us when we'd overflow our cup
That tomorrow's another day.

PATRONS OF PARASITES?

Failure to use and develop
one's God-given talents and abilities
is one of the graver sins;
and those who encourage such indolence
by subsidizing it, share a measure
of guilt for the offense.

INVITED BLISTER

Some refuse to see the light
Until scorched by its heat.

HONEYED WORDS, OR HARD?

While praise, all too often, is only flattery,
Criticism usually bears a seal of sincerity;
For an enemy will praise to get what he wants,
But a true friend criticizes where he thinks it will help.

ONLY A STARTING POINT

Wishing alone will not make them come true,
No matter how noble our dreams may be;
Their effects will be nil, unless and until
They're fulfilled through action by you and me.

MARTINETS AND MARIONETTES

One wonders whether those
whose gifts always have strings attached
are interested more in helping the recipients
or in making puppets of them.

THE MAGNETS

The bee is drawn to nectar,
The river towards the sea;
The miser's drawn to money,
And so, too, with you and me.
We each pursue things we love,
The rest we just ignore;
So knowing they've their own interests,
Why of others will we expect more?

RATHER FIGHT THAN SWITCH!

Although they may grow weary
of always being on the giving end,
not many'd willingly exchange positions
with those who need their help.

GET A LITTLE LIGHT

Just stumbling about in the dark,
one rarely finds what he seeks—
but, often enough, he stubs a toe!

SORE SPOT

When our viewpoints create unhappiness
Causing others to resist and dissent,
Re-examination may reveal, perhaps,
Our own perspective's become bent.

PAINFUL PUNCTUATION

Words are powerful weapons;
They can sway and beguile men's minds,
Yet they cannot obliterate fact.
And those too-readily convinced
By another's mere saying
That a stone wall is not there
Are not spared the cuts and bruises
When they've crashed against it.

WOOL OVER THEIR EYES!

The poor sheep has no choice about being sheared.
But many men, despite the advantages of a free will,
Permit themselves, like lambs, to be "fleeced" repeatedly.

THE ZOMBIE

One who sees a child smile yet feels no inner glow,
Who scans the book of life not caring to really know,
Who'll watch a tree grow tall and not wonder at the cause,
Who only takes from others but does not himself give love,
Is one who, though he walks and breathes and blinks his eyes,
Is not really, in his soul, alive!

SAFETY IN SILENCE

The jackass who'd pass as a horse
Must keep a closed mouth, of course,
Lest he may if he neigh
Be betrayed by a bray
And be pinned with a tail of remorse.

MIDDLE-MAN OUT!

Never commit one friend to fulfill
What you promise a second you'll do;
For he upon whom you depend
Just might not follow through.
And instead of helping one friend,
You may, in fact, have lost two!

LIFE'S SMELTER

Challenge or necessity
makes the best alloy
for testing man's mettle!

THE WRINGER'S AFTERMATH

When your facial muscles sag because you smiled
and you would rather have frowned;
When your arm feels sore because you shook the hand
of someone you wanted to slap down;
When your tongue is dry from whispering pleasantries
to one at whom you'd like to shout;
When your body aches from your painful graciousness
towards one you'd prefer to rout;
When your mind is hazy with fatigue from entertaining
those you'd have preferred to ignore;
Then you have awakened to that "morning-after"
of a night you wish had not been before!

MILESTONE

One can mark the advent of his own maturity
from that Christmas when he derives more joy
out of giving gifts than from receiving them.

A SLICE OR A LOAF?

We owe not nearly so much to the man
who lets us share his success
as to the one who shows us how
best to achieve our own.

NARCISSUS

Even as we profess our love for another,
our eyes and our hearts often glance
more lovingly towards a mirror.

MORE THAN A SKULL

Most every problem in which man's involved
Requires a thinking mind through which to be solved.
No matter how high or dense the wall,
One bright idea or plan could make it fall.
But, alas, how oft is the human head
Quite shamefully misused instead—
Not to think problems through and avoid a jam
But only as a kind of battering ram!

SUB-SURFACE EVIL

Life's greatest perils,
like those of the iceberg,
often lurk unseen
beneath a placid sea.

OUR STEWARDSHIP

In the world of nature
Time is the inevitable destroyer.
Left untended, glorious paintings fade,
Magnificent temples and statues crumble,
And mighty iron horses slow to a walk!
But, that which is precious to man—
Of his creations and of himself—
Can, to a degree, be preserved
With love and devotion by those
Who take the time to care.

DELILAH

One does not resist
the seductive advances
of a temptress
by letting her sit
in his lap!

ACTIONS SPEAK...!

We often hear that "Time will tell";
But, it has little to say
unless we lend it our voice.

EQUILIBRIUM

The sign of maturity
is the ability to take life's "ups"
without soaring into dangerous euphoria
and its "downs" without plunging
into an abyss of despair.

THE YARDSTICK

It is given to each man to live
But briefly 'mid the span of Time.
Yet the true measure of a man's life
Cannot be reckoned at all in years;
But rather in those things he's done—
Both for himself and for others,
In the things he's known and loved,
The joys and sorrows he's earned and shared.
These will measure him for all time.

COMMITTEE OF ONE

Do those things you want done now
While you're still here and can see to it;
For after you've gone, none may know how
Or be so busy they'll never get to it.

DAYS MADE GOLDEN

Though they seem to fly by
Like fenceposts past a speeding train,
Let us not lament mere passing of our years.
Let us not be troubled that we may have lived
More years than we yet will.
For what lies ahead may hold more meaning,
More happiness and contentment for us
Than all of what has gone before.
Let us, in short, remember that the sunset
Is often the most beautiful part of the day.

GRATITUDE'S GLOW

As we walk the Road of Life
At all such places as we find light
Let us pause to honor and to thank
Those who lit the candles.

✑ About The Authors ✑

Things did not come easy for Harry and Joan Mier. For each of them there was the gruelling experience of long hours, sacrifice and hard work.

Through personal initiative, ingenuity and industry, they attained the material rewards of success. And not only they, but all those who have worked along with them in their various endeavors and enterprises have profited as well.

On the day she married, Joan Mier gave up her active practice as an attorney at law to become a wife and homemaker.

Harry Mier was a pioneer in the development of one of the world's largest and most glamorous cosmetics enterprises. Since 1946, when he retired from active business at the age of 53, he and Mrs. Mier have devoted themselves to other interests they share which promised fuller meaning and deeper satisfactions in life.

Through their non-profit Harry and Joan Mier Foundation, they established 110-acre Camp Hess Kramer near Malibu, California, where an extensive program enriches the community's youth. Another oceanside camp, a low-altitude haven for crippled children further handicapped by cardiac and respiratory conditions, was donated to the Crippled Children's Society of Los Angeles County. This special facility is known as Camp Joan Mier.

The Mier's first book, *"If The Shoe Fits!"* appeared in 1959. Their widely-acclaimed *"Happiness Begins Before Breakfast"* was published in 1962 and, with printing after printing, has come to be regarded by booksellers and readers alike as a popular "standard."

In 1966, Harry and Joan Mier's third book, *"Building Our Own Rainbows,"* was published by Sherbourne Press.

Additional copies may be obtained
through your local booksellers
or be ordered direct from
Merit Publishers
P.O. Box 1344
Beverly Hills, Calif. 90213

Clothbound: Remit $3.00 plus 25¢ postage and handling.
Paperback: Remit $1.00 plus 25¢ postage and handling.
California orders add State Sales Tax.
(Above prices apply only
in U.S.A. and U.S. Territories)

Lithographed in U. S. A.—American Offset Printers, L. A.